TRUSTS MADE EASY

Smart Tools to Save Tax, Secure Wealth &

Protect Family

By

CA MOHANLAL CHHAJER

★ ★ ★

DEDICATION

To my beloved late parents —

Whose blessings, values, and sacrifices continue to inspire me every day.

This book is a tribute to your everlasting love and guidance.

About The Author

CA Mohanlal Chhajer is a seasoned Chartered Accountant with over 32 years of experience in taxation, financial planning, and wealth management. He is a recognized expert in trust formations, estate planning, and tax-saving strategies for individuals and businesses. Throughout his career, he has assisted clients in legally reducing tax liabilities, optimizing financial structures, and securing long-term wealth through the use of private trusts, Hindu Undivided Families (HUFs), and strategic tax planning. His expertise also encompasses financial transparency and governance, ensuring compliance while maximizing financial efficiency.

Beyond his professional pursuits, Mohanlal has held leadership positions in various social organizations and professional bodies, actively advocating for financial discipline and ethical management. He is a passionate speaker, mentor, and author, dedicated to educating individuals on smart tax-saving strategies and financial independence. Believing that learning is a lifelong journey, he has attended renowned programs such as Landmark Worldwide Education, Success Gyan, Tony Robbins' seminars, and sessions by Mahatria, continuously expanding his knowledge and insights.

"Trusts Made Easy: A Practical Guide for Everyday Understanding" is a culmination of Mohanlal's extensive experience, aimed at helping professionals and business owners navigate the complexities of taxation with legally sound strategies.

Experience Highlights

Over the past two decades, Mohanlal has dedicated his practice to assisting individuals and organizations in establishing various types of trusts and ensuring the seamless filing of income tax returns. His experience encompasses the creation of private trusts, navigating the complexities of the Indian Trusts Act, 1882, and adhering to the Income Tax Act, 1961.

Common Challenges in Trust Formation and Tax Filing

Throughout his career, Mohanlal has encountered several recurring challenges faced by clients during trust formation and tax filing:

1. **Ambiguity in Trust Objectives:** Unclear articulation of the trust's purpose can lead to legal complications and misinterpretation.

2. **Selection of Trustees:** Identifying trustworthy and competent individuals to manage the trust is often a daunting task.

3. **Compliance with Registration Procedures:** Navigating the bureaucratic processes involved in registering a trust can be time-consuming and complex.

4. **Accurate Income Reporting:** Ensuring precise reporting of income and adherence to tax obligations to avoid penalties.

Best Practices for Effective Trust Management

To address these challenges, Mohanlal recommends the following strategies:

- **Define Clear Objectives:** Articulate the trust's purpose explicitly in the trust deed to provide clear guidance for trustees and beneficiaries.

- **Select Qualified Trustees:** Choose individuals with integrity, financial acumen, and a commitment to the trust's objectives.

- **Ensure Thorough Documentation:** Maintain comprehensive records of all transactions, decisions, and communications related to the trust.

- **Stay Updated on Legal Requirements:** Regularly review and comply with current laws and regulations governing trusts and taxation.

Contact Information

- **Email:** mlchhajerca@gmail.com

- **Phone:** +91 94440 65508

About This Book

"Trusts Made Easy: Smart Tools to Save Tax, Secure Wealth & Protect Family" is your no-jargon, real-world road map to preserving wealth and optimizing taxes using private trusts.

Forget the complicated legal lingo — this book breaks down complex financial concepts into simple, actionable steps. Whether you're protecting ₹10 lakhs or ₹10 crores, you'll discover how private trusts can be a game-changer.

Inside, you'll learn: ☑ **Different types of trusts** – Revocable, Irrevocable, Discretionary, and Specific.

☑ **Legal aspects of trust formation** – Drafting trust deeds, understanding trustee responsibilities, and staying compliant.

☑ **Tax-saving strategies** – How trusts can legally reduce your tax burden.

☑ **Succession planning** – Transfer wealth smoothly, minus the drama.

☑ **Asset protection** – Shield your assets from legal disputes, creditors, and mismanagement.

But wait — **aren't trusts only for the rich?**

Nope. Trusts aren't just for the wealthy. They're for the wise.

Whether you own ₹10 lakhs or ₹10 crores, a private trust can help you:

📑 Legally reduce your taxes

🛡 Protect your hard-earned assets

🎭 Ensure your family gets what you intended — without the drama

⚖ Safeguard your wealth from unexpected claims or family disputes

And here's the kicker — **it's not rocket science.**

This book walks you through the entire process step by step — **without jargon, without confusion, and without the headache.**

I'm a Chartered Accountant with 32 years of experience. Over the decades, I've seen people lose money not because they were reckless — but because they simply didn't know better.

This book is my way of saying: Enough is enough.

Let's make smart tax planning simple, stress-free, and accessible for everyone.

WHY THIS BOOK? 

This book is for anyone looking to reduce their tax burden legally and plan their wealth efficiently. It is particularly useful for:

- Business Owners & Entrepreneurs – To structure wealth, protect assets, and reduce business-related tax liabilities.

- Salaried Professionals & HNIs – To create trusts for long-term wealth accumulation and minimize taxation.

- Parents & Guardians – To secure financial independence for children, especially minors, through beneficiary trusts.

- Investors & Real Estate Owners – To distribute income across trusts and lower tax exposure.

- Financial Advisors & Tax Consultants – To gain deeper insights into trust structures and guide clients effectively.

- Anyone Interested in Smart Tax Planning – To explore trust strategies and legal ways to optimize taxation.

If you want to pay less tax legally, protect your wealth, and ensure a financially secure future, this book is for you!

ACKNOWLEDGMENT

Writing this book has been an enriching journey, and I am deeply grateful to those who have supported me along the way.

First and foremost, I extend my heartfelt gratitude to my mentors, colleagues, and fellow Chartered Accountants who have shared their invaluable insights and experiences, helping shape the practical approach of this book.

A special mention to Gaurav Arora, an exceptional coach for CAs, whose guidance and mentorship have played a significant role in shaping my professional journey. His wisdom, strategic insights, and unwavering support have been instrumental in refining my approach to tax planning and wealth management.

I sincerely thank my family for their patience, encouragement, and support, especially during the late nights and long hours spent researching and writing. Their belief in my work has been my greatest motivation.

A heartfelt thanks to my clients and associates, whose real-life tax planning challenges and financial concerns inspired many of the strategies discussed in this book. Your trust and confidence in my expertise have been the driving force behind this work.

I would also like to acknowledge the pioneers in tax laws, estate planning, and trust structures, whose contributions to financial planning have paved the way for professionals like me to simplify complex concepts for a wider audience.

Lastly, a big thank you to my readers—whether you are an entrepreneur, professional, or investor—who are keen to explore legal ways to optimize taxes and secure financial stability. This book is for you, and I hope it empowers you to make informed, strategic financial decisions.

With deep appreciation,

CA Mohanlal Chhajer

DISCLAIMER

This book is intended for informational and educational purposes only. The contents herein are based on the author's professional experience, research, and interpretation of tax laws as of the date of publication.

However, tax laws, financial regulations, and legal provisions are subject to change, and readers are advised to consult a qualified Chartered Accountant, tax consultant, or legal expert before making any financial, tax, or investment decisions.

The author and publisher make no representations or warranties regarding the accuracy, completeness, or applicability of the information provided. Any reliance on the material in this book is solely at the reader's discretion and risk.

The author and publisher shall not be held responsible for any errors, omissions, or financial or legal consequences resulting from the use of this information.

Furthermore, this book does not create a professional-client relationship between the reader and the author. The examples, case studies, and strategies discussed are for illustrative purposes only and may not be applicable to every individual's financial situation.

By reading this book, you acknowledge that you are responsible for your own financial and legal decisions and agree to seek professional advice when necessary.

REAL WORDS FROM REAL PEOPLE 

1. General Chartered Accountant Services

"Working with Mr. Mohanlal Chhajer has brought a new level of clarity and confidence to my financial matters. His in-depth knowledge, practical advice, and timely responses make him a rare gem in the world of finance. I now make decisions with far more assurance thanks to his guidance."

– Anopchand Jain

2. Tax Planning & Trust Formation

"I had heard about trusts before, but never realized how much they could help in tax planning until I met Mohanlal ji. He guided me through every step—from formation to legal compliance—and helped me legally reduce my tax burden without a shred of worry. Highly recommended!"

– Jayantilal Challani

3. Beneficiary Trust Setup

"Mohanlal sir introduced me to the concept of beneficiary trusts in a way that completely changed how I look at the tax planning.His step- by -step guidance made the entire process smooth & legally sound.I feel more secure about my family's financial future thanks to his expertise"

– Sushil Lalwani

4. Multi-Generational Planning with Trusts

"I always thought tax planning was only about saving money today. But thanks to Mohanlal ji, I've created a roadmap that benefits not just me but my next generation too. His approach is practical, legal, and deeply insightful."

– P. Sunil Jain

Table Of Contents

CHAPTER 1

UNDERSTANDING TRUSTS

What Is A Trust? And Why You (Yes, You!) Should Seriously Consider One

Let Me Start With a Short Story...

A few years ago, a client—let's call him Mr. Sharma—walked into my office.

A successful businessman. Loving family. Multiple properties. But just one simple question:

"Mohanlalji, what happens to my wealth if something happens to me?"

Simple question, right?

But the consequences—without a trust—can be anything but simple.

So, let's break this down. Slowly. Clearly. And without drowning you in legal mumbo-jumbo.

What is a Trust? (No Legal Jargon, I Promise 😄)

A trust is a legal setup where you (the settlor) transfer your assets to someone you trust (the trustee) to manage on behalf of the beneficiaries—as per your instructions.

In even simpler terms:

Think of it as appointing your personal wealth manager—not just for today, but even after you're gone.

The Dream Team: Who's Involved in a Trust? (Let's Turn This into a Cricket Match 🏏)

1. Settlor (The Captain)

That's you! The one who creates the trust, sets the rules, and transfers property or money into it.

2. Trustee (The Manager)

The person or people who manage the trust assets according to your instructions.

3. Beneficiaries (The Team Players)

The people who benefit from the trust.

Who Can Become a Trustee?

Anyone who's mentally sound and not legally barred:

- You, the settlor

- A friend or family member

- A beneficiary (unless restricted)

- Chartered Accountants, lawyers, professionals

- Corporate trustees like banks

- Multiple co-trustees

- Court-appointed trustees

But not:

- Minors

- Unsound mind

- Insolvent individuals

- Convicted fraudsters

Types of Trusts (Just the Basics)

Two categories:

- Public Trusts – For charitable/religious purposes

- Private Trusts – For specific people (family/heirs)

This book focuses on Private Trusts.

When Does a Trust Come Into Effect?

- Living Trust (Inter Vivos) – While you're alive

- Will Trust (Testamentary) – After your death

What Assets Can You Put Into a Trust?

Everything you own!

- Cash, FDs, Shares, Real Estate, Insurance, Digital Assets, Gold

Pro Tip: Start small—one FD or one property.

Who Should Consider Creating a Private Trust?

Everyone! Whether you're salaried, business owner, senior citizen or parent.

Benefits:

- Reduce taxes

- Avoid disputes

- Protect family

- Easy wealth transfer

Real-Life Case: The Ramesh bhai Strategy

Two sons—one responsible, one reckless.

He created a trust, made the stable son trustee, and ensured the reckless one only got a monthly income.

Result: Peace of mind!

Why Should You Care About Trusts?

Analogy:

You = The Cook

Trustee = The Delivery Guy

Beneficiaries = The Hungry Customers

You decide:

- What's on the menu (assets)

- Who gets what

- When it's served

That's power!

Real Story: "The businessman Who Outsmarted the Taxman"

Ravi, 38, Businessman.

Worried about his wife and child.

Created trust for daughter's education & marriage.

Saved ₹70,000 tax/year. Smart parenting!

What Type of Trust Should You Create?

Goal	Ideal Trust Type
Flexibility	Revocable Trust
Protection & tax	Irrevocable Trust
Let trustee decide	Discretionary Trust
Fixed shares	Specific Trust

Final Thoughts: Trusts Aren't Just Legal Documents—They're Acts of Love

Creating a private trust says:

"Even if I'm not around, I've got your back."

It's peace of mind. A legacy. A final gift.

What You Can Do Right Now:

- List your assets

- Decide who you want to protect

- Ask: "If I'm gone, will they know what to do?"

Next Up: Chapter 2 — Meet the Trust Family: Types of Private Trusts & How to Choose the Right One for You

TYPES OF TRUSTS

Key Differences Between Various Trusts

Types of Private Trusts – Choose Your Weapon Wisely 🛡

"If you don't know where you're going, any road will get you there."

But when it comes to **trusts**, taking the wrong road can cost you… in taxes, control, and peace of mind.

Let's decode the main types of **private trusts** so you don't end up choosing a cheese burst dosa when all you really needed was a crispy masala one. 😄

🍽 Let's Meet the Trust Family

All private trusts have the same core components (settlor, trustee, beneficiaries), but their **rules**, **flexibility**, and **tax implications** vary. Think of them like different cooking styles of the same dish.

Here are the main varieties:

1. Public Charitable Trust vs. Private Beneficiary Trust

Aspects	Public Charitable Trust	Private Beneficiary Trust
Beneficiary	General public or a specific section of the society	Private individuals usually family members
Governance	Regulated by charity laws Requires trustees	Governed by trust deed Managed by trustees
Tax benefits	Exempt under 12A Donations eligible for 80G	Taxed as a separate entity No general exemptions
Income uses	Funds must be used for charitable purposes	Funds can be used for personal benefits of beneficiaries

| Compliance | Require annual filing with charity commissioner | Requires tax filings & trustee management |

2. Specific Trust vs. Discretionary Trust

Aspect	Specific Trust	Discretionary Trust
Definition	The share of each beneficiary is fixed & defined in the trust deed	The trustee has discretion to decide the share of each beneficiary
Control	Beneficiaries have a fixed right to income or assets	Trustee has full control over distribution
Tax liability	Income is taxed in the hands of the beneficiaries	Income is taxed in the hands of the trustees at the maximum marginal rate
Flexibility	Less flexible as the beneficiary's share is pre-decided	Highly flexible, allowing strategic tax planning
Purpose	Suitable for minor beneficiaries or where the share is predetermined	Suitable for asset protection & tax optimization
Legal compliance	Requires clear documentation of beneficiary's share	Requires careful drafting to avoid misuse and legal disputes

3. Revocable Trust vs. Irrevocable Trust

Feature	Revocable Trust	Irrevocable Trust
Definition	A trust where the settlor retains the right to modify or cancel the trust any time	A trust that, once created, cannot be modified or revoked by the settlor
Control	The settlor retains full control over assets and can make changes	The settlor loses control over the assets after transferring them to the trust
Taxation	Income is taxed in the hands of the settlor since they still control the trust	The trust is considered a separate taxable entity and income is taxed in the hands of the trust or beneficiaries
Asset protection	Offers little or no protection as creditors can claim against the trust assets	Provides strong asset protection, as assets are no longer considered part of the settlor's estate
Legal standing	Can be challenged easily since the settlor has control over assets	Hard to challenge, as assets are legally transferred out of the settlor's ownership

Types of Private Trusts: Explained Simply

A Revocable Trust is like holding the remote control—you, as the settlor, retain the ability to modify, amend, or even revoke the trust during your lifetime. This option offers full flexibility, especially useful if you're still charting your financial journey. However, the assets in a revocable trust are still legally considered yours.

That means they're subject to income tax in your hands and are not protected from creditor claims. The upside? It's easy to set up, gives you full control, and can be used as a backup plan in case of incapacity.

On the downside, there are no tax benefits, and asset protection is virtually nil. This type of trust is best suited for someone who wants to 'test the waters' before diving into long-term commitments.

In contrast, an Irrevocable Trust is like locking your assets in a vault—with rules that cannot be rewritten. Once the trust is created and assets are transferred, you relinquish control. The trust cannot be cancelled or altered, making this a powerful tool for asset protection, tax reduction, and long-term legacy planning. Income is no longer taxed in your hands but either in the trust or the beneficiary's hands.

It's ideal for those who are confident about their planning goals and want to protect assets from creditors, legal disputes, or future uncertainties. However, the irreversible nature requires careful thought—once done, there's no going back.

A Specific Trust can be compared to a fixed menu. The beneficiaries and their respective shares are clearly stated in the trust deed, leaving no room for interpretation. This format works well when you want absolute clarity—say, two children receiving 50% each of a particular property or income. It ensures transparency and helps avoid future disputes within the family. However, it lacks adaptability, and if situations change (like a new child or evolving needs), the trust won't accommodate them. Also, if not structured smartly, it may attract higher tax in certain cases. It's best for families where everything is already well-defined.

Lastly, the Discretionary Trust is like the chef's choice on a gourmet menu—the trustee decides how much to distribute, to whom, and when. The beneficiaries are known, but the shares are not fixed in the deed. This trust provides maximum flexibility and is particularly useful for families with young children, special needs dependents, or unpredictable financial dynamics. It also helps spread income and may reduce tax burden depending on its structuring. However, since the trustee holds significant power, it's essential to appoint someone capable and trustworthy. While beneficiaries may feel uncertain due to the lack of fixed entitlements, this format is excellent for complex or evolving family scenarios.

Each trust type serves a unique purpose. Choosing the right one depends on your goals—whether you want control, flexibility, protection, or predictability. Think of them as tools in a toolbox; pick the right one for the job.

⚖ Quick Comparison Table

Type of Trust	Can Modify?	Tax Advantage	Asset Protection	Best For
Revocable Trust	☑ Yes	✗ No	✗ No	Flexibility, short-term planning
Irrevocable Trust	✗ No	☑ Yes	☑ Yes	Long-term planning, asset protection
Specific Trust	✗ No	☑ Yes	☑ Yes	Equal division, clarity in distribution
Discretionary Trust	☑ Trustee decides	⚠ Maybe	☑ Yes	Flexible planning, unpredictable situations

🔍 Real Life Scenarios

👥 **Scenario A**

Rajesh has three children—two are settled, one is still in college.

He chooses a **discretionary trust** so the trustee can give more to the child still studying, and adjust later.

🏠 **Scenario B**

Sonal owns a flat and wants it to go 100% to her daughter after her passing.

She sets up a **specific trust** with her daughter as the only beneficiary.

👨‍👧 **Scenario C**

Mahesh has a complicated family and fears legal disputes.

He creates an **irrevocable trust** to lock assets away and avoid court cases later.

🧠 How to Choose the Right One?

Ask yourself:

☑ Do I want flexibility, or am I ready to lock it in?

☑ Do I trust someone else to take decisions on behalf of my family?

☑ Am I more focused on tax saving or control?

☑ Will my beneficiaries be able to handle wealth wisely?

Final Thought for This Chapter

Choosing the right type of trust is like picking the right luggage for a world tour—choose the wrong one, and you'll find yourself frustrated at every checkpoint. It's not just about storing wealth, it's about carrying it smartly through life's journey.

If flexibility is your top priority, a revocable trust might be your best travel companion. It lets you make changes as your life evolves. On the other hand, if your goal is to ensure asset protection and enjoy tax efficiency, then an irrevocable trust is your true friend.

Looking to distribute wealth in fixed, clear proportions among beneficiaries? That's where a specific trust comes in—it's neat, straightforward, and leaves little room for confusion. But if you want to retain some decision-making power while still planning smartly for taxes, a discretionary trust gives you that edge.

There's no one-size-fits-all when it comes to trusts. The best choice depends on your personal, financial, and family dynamics. But with the guidance offered throughout this book, you'll gain the clarity and confidence needed to choose what suits your goals best.

Remember: Trusts aren't about giving up control—they're about giving the right control to the right people, at the right time.

In the next chapter, we'll break down how to actually create a trust—from drafting the deed to registering it, and all the smart things you should include. Ready to turn planning into action? Let's go!

Chai or coffee  (or both!).

★ ★ ★ ★

CHAPTER 3

TAX IMPLICATIONS OF TRUSTS

Tax Planning Vs. Tax Avoidance Vs. Tax Evasion — Know The Difference Before The Taxman Knows You

Most people hear the word "tax" and immediately think of stress, paperwork, and a black hole called "Income Tax Department." But did you know there's a legal and brilliant way to *reduce* your tax liability *without* running from the authorities?

Before we dive deeper into private trusts and their tax-saving magic, let's first clear the fog around three commonly misunderstood terms:

👉 **Tax Planning,**

👉 **Tax Avoidance,** and

👉 **Tax Evasion.**

Let's decode these one by one—with zero jargon and a little fun.

☑ Tax Planning – The Legal Cheat Code 🧠

This is the good guy in the story. Tax planning is all about arranging your financial affairs in such a way that you pay the **least tax possible—legally**.

It's like shopping during Diwali sales—you get the same stuff, but with discounts!

✓ Uses deductions, exemptions, rebates, and smart structures like **private trusts**

✓ Fully compliant with the Income Tax Act

✓ Actually encouraged by tax authorities

🔨 **Example:**

Mr. Shah forms a private trust for his two minor children. He allocates ₹9,00,000 to the trusts. The trusts file their own returns and claim rebates under Section 87A. Tax saved = ₹2.5+ lakhs.

Now that's smart parenting... and smarter tax planning.

🚨 Tax Avoidance – The Shady Shortcut 🔗

This one's a grey area—legal, but walking a very thin line.

Tax avoidance means finding **loopholes** or grey zones in tax laws to reduce liability. It's like hiding behind the rules, not breaking them—but the taxman is watching. 👮

⚠ May be legal

⚠ Often seen as unethical

⚠ Can lead to scrutiny, litigation, and law changes

🔨 **Example:**

A person transfers income-generating assets to a trust but still controls everything behind the scenes. On paper, it's the trust's income. In reality, it's a trick.

Let's just say—if you're playing this game, don't blame anyone when the rules change.

❌ Tax Evasion – The Dangerous Game 🔥

This is straight-up illegal. It's like playing hide-and-seek with the Income Tax Department... but they always find you.

! Involves hiding income, creating fake expenses, or using cash to dodge taxes

! Punishable with fines, penalties, and even jail time

! Zero tolerance

⚖️ **Example:**

Keeping income in offshore accounts and never reporting it? That's not tax planning—it's inviting a date with the Enforcement Directorate. 🕵️

💡 The Power of Tax Planning with Trusts

Now that we know who's the hero and who's the villain, let's return to our favorite topic—**Private Trusts**—and how they can be used as a rock-solid tax planning tool.

Here's what you can achieve through trusts:

🔐 **Asset Protection:** Especially with irrevocable and discretionary trusts

📊 **Income Splitting:** Distribute income to beneficiaries and lower total family tax

📁 **Estate Planning:** Smooth transfer of wealth across generations

👪 **HUF Integration:** Create structured financial pools for family benefit

---

🚦 When Do Trusts Pay Tax at the Maximum Marginal Rate (MMR)?

Ah, the big monster in the room—**MMR (42.744%)**, the highest tax rate in India.

Certain types of trusts can accidentally (or unknowingly) walk into the MMR trap. Let's break it down.

🔖 Cases Where Trusts Pay Tax at MMR:

Discretionary Trusts (Indeterminate Beneficiaries):

When the beneficiaries and their shares are not clearly defined.

"Who will get how much? Let's decide later."

→ Taxed at MMR.

2️⃣ Trusts with Business Income:

Unless the business is incidental and separate books are maintained,

→ MMR applies.

3️⃣ Income Not Allocated to Beneficiaries:

If the income is just sitting there, not distributed or assigned,

→ MMR again.

4️⃣ Revocable Trusts:

If the settlor can reclaim the assets,

→ The income is taxed in their own hands—likely at MMR.

☑️ When Can a Trust *Avoid* MMR?

This is where the magic begins:

💡 If your trust has **clearly defined beneficiaries** with **specific shares**, the income is taxed in *their* hands as per *their individual tax slabs*.

That's right—if planned properly, **each beneficiary can enjoy the basic exemption limit and Section 87A rebate**, bringing their tax to *zero*. 😊

Mr. Sudhir's Tax Planning Masterstroke: A Real-Life Scenario

👨‍💼 **About Mr. Sudhir:**

> **Gross Business Income**: ₹20,00,000
>
> **Family**: Two minor children
>
> **Smart Move**: Created 2 private trusts and allocated ₹4.75 lakhs to each

---

▦ **Tax Comparison (FY 2024–25)**

Particulars	Old Regime *Without Trusts*	Old Regime *With Trusts*	New Regime *Without Trusts*	New Regime *With Trusts*
Gross Income	₹20,00,000	₹10,50,000	₹20,00,000	₹10,50,000
Deductions (80C & 80D)	₹2,00,000	₹2,00,000	✕ Not Allowed	✕ Not Allowed

Taxable Income	₹18,00,000	₹8,50,000	₹20,00,000	₹10,50,000
Income Tax	₹3,50,000	₹80,000	₹3,00,000	₹67,500
Cess @ 4%	₹14,000	₹3,200	₹12,000	₹2,700
Total Tax Payable	₹3,64,000	₹83,200	₹3,12,000	₹70,200
Each Trust's Tax	—	₹0 (Income below ₹5L; Sec 87A)	—	₹0 (Income below ₹5L; Sec 87A)
Total Family Tax	₹3,64,000	₹83,200	₹3,12,000	₹70,200
Savings vs Old Regime	—	₹2,80,800	₹	₹2,41,800

💥 Conclusion:

Mr. Sudhir legally saved ₹2.81 lakhs and ₹2.41 lakhs in a single year through trust-based planning —

No shortcuts, no loopholes, just smart application of tax law! 🧠💼

🔚 Conclusion: Don't Just Pay Tax—Plan It

Mr. Sudhir didn't evade tax. He didn't exploit loopholes.

He just played smart using the law's own tools—and trusts are one of the best.

Trusts offer flexibility, privacy, control, and a beautiful way to protect and distribute wealth while reducing the tax bite.

But remember: **structure matters.** The wrong kind of trust, or poor drafting, can land you in the MMR zone.

☞ Always work with a tax professional (like yourself 😄) to get the setup right. When done properly, **trusts can turn your tax pain into a financial gain**

The Tax Optimization Magic Show – Legally Pay Less Tax

It may not involve a wand or top hat, but the use of private trusts in tax planning often feels nothing short of magical when applied correctly. Let's explore how a well-structured trust can reduce your tax liability—legally and efficiently.

One of the key goals of using private trusts is to split income, avoid clubbing provisions, and optimize the use of tax slabs across family members.

One powerful strategy is creating an irrevocable trust for the benefit of a minor child. Normally, a minor's income is clubbed with the income of the parent and taxed at the parent's slab rate. However, when you set up an irrevocable trust for the minor, the income earned by the trust is assessed in the hands of the trust itself, not the parent. This means the trust can claim the basic exemption limit independently. For instance, if the trust earns ₹2.5 lakhs and has no other income, the tax payable is zero.

Another advantage lies in how private trusts are taxed. Specific or discretionary trusts are generally assessed at the slab rates applicable to individuals, not at the higher rates applicable to firms or companies. This opens the door to using the ₹2.5 lakh exemption, followed by lower slabs of 5%, 10%, and 15%. For high-net-worth individuals, this can be a significant benefit—why pay 30% plus surcharge when you can plan and bring it down to 10% through proper structuring?

Moreover, trusts offer scalability. Each trust is considered a separate legal entity with its own PAN and basic exemption limit. This means you can create multiple trusts for your children or grandchildren, spreading the income efficiently and minimizing the overall family tax burden. Of course, moderation and genuine intent are crucial—the idea is not to pull endless rabbits from the hat, but to ensure documentation and purpose are sound.

Trusts also offer strong asset protection. Assets placed into an irrevocable discretionary trust are no longer considered the personal property of either the settlor or the beneficiary. This effectively ring-fences them from legal disputes, creditors, and even tax litigation—provided the source of funds is legitimate and proper documentation, including fair market value, is maintained. The best part? Income from such protected assets—be it interest, dividends, or capital gains—continues to grow safely for the benefit of the next generation.

Lastly, the trust structure can help avoid capital gains on transfer of assets. When an asset is transferred into a revocable trust, clubbing provisions apply, and capital gains may arise. However, if the transfer is into an irrevocable trust without any consideration, it is not considered a 'transfer' under Section 47(iii) of the Income Tax Act, thereby avoiding capital gains altogether.

In conclusion, while trusts may not involve real magic, their power to reduce taxes, protect assets, and structure wealth efficiently is very real—when done right.

Quick Recap:

Trust Type	Clubbing?	Tax Slab	Capital Gain on Setup?
Revocable Trust	Yes	Settlor's	Yes
Irrevocable Specific	No	Beneficiary's	No (Sec 47(iii))

Irrevocable Discretionary	No	Trust's	No (Sec 47(iii))

Boom!  That's how the tax magician pulls legal benefits out of a humble trust hat.

In the next chapter, we'll break down **how to actually create a trust**—from drafting the deed to registering it, and all the smart things you should include.

Ready to turn your planning into action? Let's go!

★ ★ ★ ★

CHAPTER 4

ESTABLISHING A TRUST

How To Form A Private Trust Without Losing Sleep Or Money

"A goal without a plan is just a wish."

And a trust without a proper deed is just a fancy idea with no legal power.

Let's roll up our sleeves and get this thing done like a pro (without sounding like a legal textbook). 💪

Step 1: Understand WHY You're Forming the Trust

Before you dive in, ask yourself:

☑ Is it for tax saving?

☑ For asset protection from future risks (creditors, disputes, etc.)?

☑ For succession planning (to pass assets to children or other family members smoothly)?

☑ For a specific goal like education, medical care, or maintaining a property?

Your why will decide your how—so don't skip this part.

Step 2: Drafting the Trust Deed – The Soul of the Trust

This is the main document—like the constitution of your trust. It should be clear, complete, and compliant.

📃 **Basic Ingredients:**

Name of the Trust – e.g., Aashish *Family Trust*

Date of Creation

Name of Settlor – the person creating the trust (you!)

Name(s) of Trustee(s) – those who'll manage the trust

Initial Contribution – even ₹100 is fine to start with

Beneficiaries – who'll receive the benefits

Purpose of the Trust – must be clearly defined

Type of Trust – revocable, irrevocable, specific, discretionary

🧂 Optional but Smart Add-ons:

How income will be distributed

Rules on adding/removing beneficiaries

Power to amend (for revocable trusts only)

Succession plan for trustee(s)

Investment powers of the trustee

Restrictions (like "no distribution until age 21")

🧠 **Pro Tip:** Don't copy-paste a deed from the internet blindly. Every trust is like a tailor-made suit—one size never fits all.

Step 3: Contribute Assets

To bring your trust to life, you must transfer some property (called "corpus") into it. This can be:

Cash (start with ₹100 or more)

Bank deposits

Shares or mutual funds

Land or building

Gold or even intellectual property

🔐 *Important:* Once you transfer assets to an irrevocable trust, they are no longer legally yours. Choose wisely.

"Transferring assets to a trust is like giving your kids access to your Netflix account—be generous, but know it's out of your hands now!"

Step 4: Get It Signed and Registered

For movable property (cash, shares, etc.):

No registration is mandatory

A signed trust deed on non-judicial stamp paper (usually worth 4% of the corpus value, varies by state)

For immovable property (land, house, flat):

Must be registered at the local Sub-Registrar office

Pay stamp duty based on state law

👍 Make sure all parties sign in front of two witnesses

📝 *Tip:* Never copy a deed from Google like it's a recipe for pasta. Trusts are tailor-made legal documents, not one-size-fits-all meals.

Step 5: Apply for PAN of the Trust

Like every living entity in India, your trust needs its own PAN card.

File Form 49A online via NSDL/UTIITSL and upload a scanned copy of:

Trust deed

PAN & Aadhaar of trustee(s)

Address proof of trust

🗣 Tip: Use the trust's name and not any individual's name in bank accounts or tax filings.

Step 6: Open a Bank Account in Trust's Name

Visit your preferred bank with:

Trust deed (original + copy)

PAN of the trust

KYC of trustees

Resolution signed by all trustees (mentioning who is authorized to operate the account)

Now the trust is fully operational—you can start receiving income, making investments, or distributing benefits.

Step 7: Maintain Books & File Returns

Yes, your trust is now a separate entity. It must:

Maintain books of account

File ITR-5 annually

Deduct and deposit TDS if applicable

File Form 10 if claiming exemptions (for charitable trusts)

📑 *For private family trusts, tax planning is key.* We'll dive into those juicy details in Chapter 5.

✖ Common Mistakes to Avoid

Naming minor children as trustees (only adults can act)

Not mentioning "irrevocable" in an irrevocable trust deed

Not updating address or PAN in case of changes

Ignoring the power of trustees—either too much or too little

Forgetting to register if immovable property is involved

Real Example:

Suresh creates a trust to ensure smooth distribution of rental income from 3 flats between his two children.

He names himself the initial trustee, and includes a clause for automatic replacement with his brother if he becomes incapable.

He starts with ₹1,000 as initial corpus, drafts the deed clearly, gets it notarized, and opens a trust bank account.

His CA handles PAN application and yearly filings.

Simple. Clean. Stress-free.

🎉 You Did It!

Setting up a private trust may sound like climbing Everest, but with the right guide ( hello), it's more like a pleasant uphill hike—with beautiful views of tax savings and peace of mind.

★ ★ ★ ★

CHAPTER 5

MANAGING AND OPERATING A TRUST

Operation & Management Of The Trust

Now that your trust is alive and kicking (congrats 🎉), let's make sure it doesn't turn into a legal zombie 🧟 later. Good record-keeping and responsible trusteeship are like regular checkups for your trust's health.

Step 1: Record Keeping & Accounts

- Maintain **books of accounts** to track inflows and outflows.

- File **income tax returns (ITR)** annually.

- Conduct **audit (if applicable)**.

Step 2: Investments & Fund Management

- Ensure investments comply with **trust deed and legal restrictions**.

- Distribute income to beneficiaries as per the trust deed.

Step 3: Compliance & Legal Obligations

- File **annual reports** for charitable trusts.

- Adhere to **Trust Act, Income Tax Act, and other relevant laws**.

- Think of this as the boring but necessary grown-up stuff. Trusts may save taxes, but they don't come with autopilot.

Modify trust deed (if needed) following the legal procedure.

"Transferring assets to a trust is like giving your kids access to your Netflix account—be generous, but know it's out of your hands now!"

How a Trust Gets Income & Contributions

A trust can receive funds through various sources, depending on whether it is a private trust or a public (charitable/religious) trust.

1. Contributions from Settlor & Beneficiaries

- The settlor (creator of the trust) contributes the initial corpus to establish the trust.

- Beneficiaries or other individuals may voluntarily contribute to the trust.

2. Rental Income

- If the trust owns land, buildings, or other properties, it can earn rental income from leasing them out.

3. Investment Income

- Trusts may earn interest, dividends, or capital gains from investments in fixed deposits, mutual funds, or securities.

4. Business Activities (Only for Charitable Trusts)

- Some charitable trusts run educational institutions, hospitals, or training centers, generating income.

- However, business income must be used for charitable purposes to retain tax-exempt status.

5. Membership Fees & Subscriptions

- Some trusts charge membership fees from members or recurring subscription fees for services.

6. Royalty, Copyright, or Intellectual Property Income

- If the trust owns patents, copyrights, or trademarks, it can earn income through royalties and licensing fees.

Where Can a Trust Invest?

The investment options depend on whether the trust is private or public:

☑ Safe & Legally Permitted Investments (for Both Private & Public Trusts)

- Fixed Deposits (FDs) with Scheduled Banks

- Government Bonds & Securities

- Mutual Funds (Debt & Index Funds Recommended for Stability)

- Corporate Bonds (AAA-rated for Safety)

- Real Estate (Rental or Long-term Asset Growth)

🚫 Restricted or Risky Investments

- Stock Market Speculation (High Risk) – Allowed for private trusts but should be carefully managed.

Conclusion

- A trust can generate income through contributions, investments, rent, and business activities (if allowed). It should invest wisely in safe and legally permitted assets to maintain financial stability.

- When Does a Trust Have to Pay Tax at the Maximum Marginal Rate (MMR)?

- A trust is generally taxed based on its structure and purpose. However, in certain situations, it is liable to pay tax at the Maximum Marginal Rate (MMR), which is 42.744% (including surcharge & cess) in India.

- **Final Thought:** Make Your Trust Work *For* You, Not *Against* You

CHAPTER 6

DRAFTING A TRUST DEED

You wouldn't build a house on sand. Likewise, don't build your trust on a shaky document. The trust deed is your Constitution, your playbook, your family's secret sauce recipe. Get it right the first time.

Drafting a Trust Deed is a critical step in setting up a trust, as it governs the rights, duties, and obligations of the settlor, trustees, and beneficiaries. Here are some key precautions to take:

1. Clarity in Objectives & Purpose

- Clearly define the purpose of the trust (e.g., family wealth management, tax planning, charity, etc.).

- Ensure that the objectives comply with legal and tax regulations.

- Avoid vague language that can create confusion or disputes.

-

2. Precise Definition of Key Roles

☑ **Settlor: Clearly state the name and contribution of the settlor.**

☑ **Trustees:**

- Appoint reliable and competent trustees.

- Define their powers, responsibilities, and limitations clearly.

- Mention whether trustees have the right to appoint successors.

- Specify conflict of interest clauses to prevent misuse of power.

☑ **Beneficiaries:**

- Clearly define who qualifies as a beneficiary.

- In a discretionary trust, specify how trustees will distribute income.

- For minors, specify how funds will be managed until they reach adulthood.

3. Corpus & Fund Management

- Clearly mention the initial contribution (corpus) and provisions for adding funds in the future.

- Specify investment options and restrictions (e.g., no speculative investments).

- Define how the income will be used or reinvested.

4. Tax & Legal Compliance

- Ensure the trust structure complies with Indian Trusts Act, 1882 (for private trusts) or relevant state laws (for public trusts).

- For tax benefits, draft the deed in accordance with Income Tax Act, 1961 (e.g., 12A & 80G for charitable trusts).

- Include clubbing provisions if minor beneficiaries are involved (to avoid unintended taxation).

- Mention whether the trust is revocable or irrevocable, as revocable trusts may be taxed in the hands of the settlor.

5. Distribution & Dissolution Clauses

- Define how and when the trust property will be distributed to beneficiaries.

- In case of trust termination, specify how the remaining assets will be disposed of.

- For charitable trusts, state that assets will be transferred to another registered trust (not individuals) upon dissolution.

6. Dispute Resolution & Amendments

- Include a dispute resolution mechanism (e.g., arbitration or mediation) to avoid costly litigation.

- Specify if and how the trust deed can be amended in the future.

7. Proper Execution & Registration

- Execute the trust deed on adequate stamp paper (as per state stamp duty rules).

- Register the trust deed if it involves immovable property (mandatory under Registration Act, 1908).

- Ensure it is signed by the settlor, trustees, and at least two witnesses.

Taking these precautions will ensure the trust is legally valid, tax-efficient, and protected from disputes.

PRO TIP: Have a lawyer and a CA review your deed — even if you've read every word. Trusts are long-term, and any small error now can cause big headaches later.

CHAPTER 7

DISSOLVING A TRUST

Dissolving a Trust – When It's Time to Say Goodbye

Like all good things (ice cream, vacations, and superhero movies), some trusts must come to an end. But unlike breakups, dissolving a trust must follow proper legal rituals.

When Can a Trust be Dissolved?

A trust can be **dissolved** under the following circumstances:

1. As per Trust Deed (Predefined Termination Clause)

- If the trust deed **specifies a fixed duration**, the trust will dissolve when that period expires.

- If the **purpose of the trust is fulfilled**, the trust may be terminated.

- If there is a **specific event** (e.g., death of the last beneficiary), the trust ends.

2. By Consent of Beneficiaries (Private Trusts Only)

- A private trust can be dissolved if **all beneficiaries agree,** provided:

  o The trust is **not created for unborn beneficiaries**.

  o The trust **is not irrevocable**.

3. By Trustees (Under Legal or Practical Necessity)

- If managing the trust becomes **impossible or illegal,** trustees may decide to dissolve it.

- Example: If a **charitable trust loses funding** and cannot operate, it may be dissolved.

4. By Court Order

- A trust can be **legally terminated by a court** if:

  o The trust's purpose has **failed or become impossible**.

  o The trust is involved in **fraud or mismanagement**.

  o There are legal disputes leading to the trust being **declared void**.

5. On Violation of Law (Compulsory Dissolution)

- If a trust **violates the law**, such as engaging in illegal activities, the government or a court may **forcefully dissolve it**.

Process of Dissolving a Trust

1. **Pass a Resolution** – Trustees and/or beneficiaries pass a resolution approving dissolution.

2. **Settle Liabilities** – Clear all outstanding debts, taxes, and liabilities.

3. **Distribute Remaining Assets** –

   - **Private Trust** – Assets are distributed as per the trust deed.

   - **Public Trust** – Assets must be transferred to another registered charitable trust (not individuals).

4. **File for Closure with Authorities** –

   - Submit relevant documents to **Charity Commissioner (for public trusts)**.

   - Apply for **PAN cancellation** with the Income Tax Department.

5. **Legal Compliance & Tax Filings** – Final tax returns and compliance filings must be completed before closure.

ADDITIONAL ADVANTAGES OF TRUSTS

Non-Tax Benefits of Private Trusts

imagine Ramesh, a successful businessman, who suddenly finds himself in a legal battle with creditors.

Thankfully, years ago, he set up a private trust. His family's future? Untouched. His assets? Protected. That's the power of a well-structured trust.

Private trusts offer several advantages beyond just tax benefits. Here are some key non-tax advantages of private trusts:

1. Asset Protection

☑ Shield Against Creditors – Assets in a trust are protected from creditors of the settlor or beneficiaries.

☑ Protection from Legal Claims – In case of litigation, business risks, or bankruptcy, trust assets remain safeguarded.

☑ Safeguarding Against Family Disputes – Helps in preventing asset misuse or disputes among family members.

2. Wealth Preservation & Succession Planning

☑ Ensures Smooth Inheritance – Unlike a will, a trust ensures seamless transfer of wealth without probate delays.

☑ Control Over Distribution – The settlor can define conditions on how and when beneficiaries receive funds.

☑ Prevents Fragmentation of Wealth – Assets can be held and managed efficiently instead of being divided among multiple heirs.

3. Privacy & Confidentiality

☑ Not Publicly Disclosed – Unlike wills, which become public documents after death, trusts remain private.

☑ Discreet Wealth Management – Ideal for high-net-worth individuals who want to keep financial matters confidential.

4. Governance & Financial Discipline

☑ Trustees Oversee Management – Reduces the risk of reckless spending by beneficiaries.

☑ Financial Security for Minors & Dependents – Trusts can provide structured financial support to children, elderly parents, or individuals with special needs.

☑ Prevents Misuse of Inheritance – Funds can be released periodically or for specific purposes like education, marriage, or medical needs.

5. Continuity & Perpetuity

☑ Trust Can Exist Indefinitely – Unlike individuals, a trust does not "die" and can manage wealth across generations.

☑ Business Succession – Helps business owners pass on assets while maintaining continuity and avoiding disputes.

6. Customization & Flexibility

☑ Multiple Structures Available – Can be structured as discretionary, specific, revocable, or irrevocable based on needs.

☑ Can Hold Diverse Assets – Can include property, shares, bank deposits, jewelry, intellectual property, etc.

7. Avoiding Probate & Legal Hassles

☑ No Probate Required – Unlike wills, which need court validation, trusts immediately transfer assets to beneficiaries.

☑ Reduces Legal Challenges – Wills can be contested, but well-structured trusts provide strong legal protection.

CHAPTER 9

MULTIPLE TRUSTS FOR THE SAME BENEFICIARY

For example, one trust could be for a child's education and another for managing inherited property.

Absolutely, you can establish multiple private trusts benefiting the same individual. This strategy is often employed to manage diverse assets or to achieve specific financial objectives. However, it's crucial to approach this with caution.

The Income Tax Department is vigilant about such arrangements and has provisions to prevent potential tax avoidance. For instance, under Section 166 of the Income Tax Act, the Assessing Officer has the authority to assess income either in the hands of the trust or directly in the hands of the beneficiary, depending on the circumstances.

Moreover, the tax implications for income arising from these trusts depend on factors such as the trust's structure (specific or discretionary), the determinacy of beneficiaries' shares, and the nature of the income. Therefore, while setting up multiple private trusts for the same beneficiary is permissible, it's essential to consult with a tax professional to ensure compliance with tax laws and to fully understand the implications.

FREQUENTLY ASKED QUESTIONS

1. What is a private trust?

A private trust is a legal arrangement where an individual (the **grantor** or **settlor**) transfers assets to a **trustee**, who manages them for the benefit of specific individuals or entities (the **beneficiaries**). Think of it as a **financial babysitter** for your assets, ensuring they're handled according to your wishes.

****

2. How does a private trust differ from a public trust?

A **private trust** benefits specific individuals or groups (e.g., family members).

A **public trust** serves charitable or public causes, benefiting society at large.

It's like the difference between **hosting a family dinner** and **organizing a community feast!**

****

3. What are the main types of private trusts?

Private trusts come in several flavors:

Revocable Trusts: Can be altered or canceled during the grantor's lifetime.

Irrevocable Trusts: Once created, they cannot be easily changed, offering tax benefits and asset protection.

Testamentary Trusts: Created through a will and activated upon death.

Living Trusts: Established during the grantor's lifetime, managing assets before and after death.

Each type serves a different purpose—like **compartments in a well-organized financial toolbox!**

****

4. Why should someone consider setting up a private trust?

A private trust can help:

- ✔ **Manage and protect assets** – Useful for minors or financially inexperienced beneficiaries.

- ✔ **Avoid probate** – Ensures a smoother, faster transfer of assets.

- ✔ **Maintain privacy** – Unlike wills, trusts are not public records.

- ✔ **Plan for incapacity** – Ensures assets are managed if you become unable to do so.

A private trust is like a **Swiss Army knife**—versatile and useful in various financial situations.

****

5. Who are the key parties involved in a private trust?

A private trust typically includes:

Grantor (Settlor): Creates the trust.

Trustee: Manages the trust assets.

Beneficiaries: Those who benefit from the trust.

It's like a **theatrical production**—the grantor writes the script, the trustee directs the play, and the beneficiaries enjoy the performance.

****

6. Can a private trust be modified or revoked?

It depends on the trust type:

Revocable Trusts: Yes, they can be modified or revoked during the grantor's lifetime.

Irrevocable Trusts: Generally, no—once set up, changes are difficult (so choose wisely!).

****

7. Do I still need a will if I have a private trust?

Yes! A **will** covers any assets **not included** in the trust and handles matters like appointing guardians for minor children.

Think of your **trust and will as a dynamic duo**, working together to ensure your wishes are fully honored.

1.   Are private trusts only for wealthy individuals?

2. **A:** Not at all! You don't need to own a palace to need a lock on your door. Similarly, anyone who wants to protect their assets or avoid future disputes can benefit from a trust.

! While popular among the wealthy, trusts benefit anyone looking to:

- ☑ Protect their assets

- ☑ Ensure smooth inheritance planning

- ☑ Maintain privacy

It's not about **how much wealth you have**, but **how you want it managed**.

****

8. How are private trusts taxed?

Taxation varies based on **trust type and jurisdiction**:

Revocable Trusts: Usually offer **no tax advantages** during the grantor's lifetime.

Irrevocable Trusts: May provide **tax benefits**, depending on the structure.

It's best to consult a tax professional to understand your **specific situation**.

****

9. How do I set up a private trust?

✔ **Define your objectives** – Why do you want a trust?

✔ **Choose the trust type** – Revocable, irrevocable, testamentary, etc.

✔ **Select a trustee** – A trustworthy individual or institution.

✔ **Draft the trust document** – Work with a legal professional.

✔ **Fund the trust** – Transfer assets into it.

Creating a trust is like **baking a cake**—you need the **right ingredients** and a **good recipe** to get the desired outcome.

****

10. What assets can be placed in a private trust?

Almost anything, including:

✔ Real estate

✔ Stocks & bonds

✔ Business interests

✔ Cash & bank deposits

✔ Jewelry & valuable collectibles

Think of it as **packing a suitcase** for your financial future—choose what matters most!

****

11. How does a private trust help in estate planning?

A trust helps:

Streamline asset distribution

Avoid family disputes

Reduce legal delays

Ensure wealth transfers according to your wishes

Think of it as a **GPS for your financial legacy**.

****

12. Can a private trust protect assets from creditors?

Yes! **Irrevocable trusts** can shield assets from creditors because they're **no longer owned by the grantor**.

However, if the trust was set up **fraudulently** to evade debts, courts may still allow creditors to access assets.

****

13. How do beneficiaries receive distributions from a trust?

Distribution depends on the **trust terms** and can be:

✔ **Lump sum** – Paid out all at once.

✔ **Staggered payments** – At specific intervals (e.g., annually).

✔ **Discretionary payments** – Given based on the trustee's decision.

Like a **well-managed retirement fund**, trust distributions provide **financial security over time**.

****

14. What happens if the trustee mismanages the trust?

Trustees have a **legal duty** to act in the best interests of beneficiaries. If they **mismanage assets**, beneficiaries can:

Remove the trustee

Sue for financial losses

Appoint a new trustee

****

15. Can a private trust be used for charitable giving?

While primarily for **specific beneficiaries**, a private trust **can include charitable donations**.

Alternatively, a **separate charitable trust** can be established for philanthropic purposes.

****

16. How long can a private trust last?

Trust duration depends on **its terms and local laws**:

Some trusts **end when beneficiaries reach a certain age**.

Others can **last for multiple generations**, ensuring long-term financial stability.

Some jurisdictions impose a **rule against perpetuities**, limiting trusts to **80-100 years**.

****

17. Can a trustee also be a beneficiary?

Yes! A trustee **can also be a beneficiary**, but **conflict of interest rules** apply.

For example, if a trustee has **too much control** over distributions, the trust may **lose its protective benefits** (especially for tax and asset protection purposes).

****

18. Can a private trust own a business?

Yes! A trust **can hold shares** in a company, ensuring:

Smooth succession planning

Asset protection

Minimized inheritance disputes

Many **wealthy families** use trusts to **own and manage businesses**.

****

19. Can a private trust be dissolved?

Yes, under these conditions:

The **trust purpose is fulfilled**.

All beneficiaries agree to terminate it.

The **trust deed allows for dissolution**.

A **court orders its termination**.

****

20. Do private trusts need to file tax returns?

Yes, if the trust earns **taxable income** (e.g., rent, dividends, interest), it may need to **file tax returns** annually.

Taxation rules vary, so consulting a tax expert is **essential**.

****

Remember, creating a trust is like baking a cake—you need the right ingredients and a good recipe to ensure it turns out as intended.

I hope this sheds some light on the world of private trusts. Remember, while this information provides a general overview, it's always best to consult with legal and financial professionals to tailor a plan to your unique circumstances.

Asset Protection – A strategy to safeguard assets from creditors, lawsuits, or financial risks, often using trusts.

Asset Transfer – The process of legally moving assets from one entity to another, such as placing assets into a trust.

Beneficiary – A person or entity entitled to receive benefits from a trust.

Corpus of Trust – The principal or body of assets held within a trust.

Charitable Trust – A trust set up for philanthropic purposes, benefiting public welfare causes.

Discretionary Trust – A trust where the trustee has full discretion over asset distribution to beneficiaries.

Dynasty Trust – A long-term trust designed to pass wealth across multiple generations.

Estate Planning – The process of managing and distributing assets after death through legal tools like wills and trusts.

Executor – A person appointed in a will to manage and distribute the deceased's estate.

Fiduciary Duty – The legal obligation of trustees to act in the best interests of beneficiaries.

Grantor (Settlor) – The person who creates and funds a trust.

Irrevocable Trust – A trust that, once created, cannot generally be altered or revoked.

Power of Attorney (POA) – A legal document allowing an individual to act on another person's behalf in legal and financial matters.

Probate – The legal process of validating a will and distributing assets upon death.

Revocable Trust – A trust that can be modified or terminated by the grantor during their lifetime.

Successor Trustee – A trustee who takes over trust management after the initial trustee resigns, becomes incapacitated, or passes away.

Trustee – The person or entity entrusted with managing the trust's assets in the best interests of the beneficiaries."

SAMPLE TRUST DEED

This Deed of Trust is executed on this ___ day of __________, **20,** by **[Grantor's Name]**, residing at **[Grantor's Address]** (hereinafter referred to as the "Settlor"), in favor of **[Trust Name]**, a private trust created for the benefit of the beneficiaries mentioned herein.

1. Definitions

a. **Settlor:** The person establishing the trust.

b. **Trustee:** The individual/entity responsible for managing trust assets.

c. **Beneficiary:** The person(s) entitled to benefit from the trust.

d. **Trust Property:** The assets transferred into the trust.

2. Name of the Trust

The trust shall be known as **"[Trust Name]"** (hereinafter referred to as "the Trust").

3. Purpose of the Trust

The trust is established for the benefit of **[names of beneficiaries]** for the purpose of **[state purpose, e.g., asset protection, wealth distribution, education, etc.]**.

4. Trust Corpus

The Settlor transfers the following assets to the Trust as its initial corpus:

[List of assets, e.g., real estate, bank deposits, stocks, bonds, etc.]

5. Appointment of Trustee

The Settlor appoints **[Trustee's Name]**, residing at **[Trustee's Address]**, as the first trustee. The trustee shall act in accordance with the terms of this Trust Deed.

6. Powers and Duties of the Trustee

The Trustee shall:

a) Manage the trust assets prudently.

b) Make distributions to the beneficiaries as per the trust terms.

c) Invest trust funds in safe and legally permissible investments.

d) Maintain proper books of accounts for the Trust.

7. Beneficiaries

The beneficiaries of this trust shall be:

1.

[Name] (Relationship: [e.g., son/daughter/spouse])

[Name] (Relationship: [e.g., grandson/granddaughter/relative])

8. Distribution of Trust Assets

The trust assets shall be distributed as follows:

a) **Lump sum distribution** of ____% at the age of ____.

b) **Periodic distributions** for education, medical needs, and maintenance.

9. Termination of the Trust

This trust shall terminate upon the occurrence of the following events:

a) When the beneficiaries reach the age of ____ years.

b) Upon complete distribution of the trust assets.

10.Irrevocability/Revocability Clause

This Trust shall be [revocable/irrevocable], and the Settlor shall [retain/no longer retain] rights over the Trust property after its creation."

11. Governing Law

This Trust Deed shall be governed by and interpreted under the laws of **[Country/State]**.

12. Miscellaneous

a) The trustee shall not use trust assets for personal benefits.

b) In case of a dispute, arbitration shall be conducted as per [Arbitration Clause].

IN WITNESS WHEREOF, the parties hereto have executed this Trust Deed as of the date first mentioned above.

Settlor:

(Signature) ______________________________

Name: ___________________________________

Trustee:

(Signature) _______________________

Name: _____________________________

Witnesses:

1.

Signature: ________________ Name: ________________

This is a basic trust deed template. You may need to customize it based on legal requirements and specific objectives.

APPENDIX 2

Difference Between a Will and a Private Trust

Understanding the distinction between a Will and a Private Trust is vital when planning the distribution and protection of assets. While both are legal instruments used in estate planning, they serve different purposes and offer unique benefits.

S. No.	Point of Difference	Will	Private Trust
1	When It Takes Effect	Comes into force only after the testator's death.	Can be created and be effective during the lifetime (inter vivos) or after death.
2	Probate Requirement	May require probate, especially in metropolitan cities.	No probate required.

3	Privacy	Becomes a public document upon probate.	Remains private and confidential.
4	Control Over Assets	No control post death.	Settlor can retain control or set specific directions during lifetime.
5	Distribution Delay	Can take months or years due to legal formalities.	Distribution is immediate as per the trust deed.
6	Risk of Challenge	High – often contested by family members.	Lower risk if properly drafted and executed.
7	Provision for Minors/Disabled	No structured management for minors or dependents.	Can include tailored provisions for care and management of such beneficiaries.
8	Tax Planning Use	Very limited.	Effective tool for tax planning and income splitting.
9	Asset Protection	Not effective against claims or disputes.	Offers strong protection if structured well.
10	Flexibility	Fixed after death; cannot be altered.	Can be revocable or allow modifications as per deed clauses.

| 11 | Cost of Setup | Inexpensive – usually a one-time document. | Higher cost – requires drafting, possible registration, and PAN application. |
| 12 | Maintenance & Compliance | No ongoing compliance required. | Requires maintenance of accounts, possible tax filings. |

If your estate is simple and your family harmonious, a Will may suffice. But if you're looking for greater control, asset protection, support for vulnerable dependents, or tax efficiency, a Private Trust is a powerful option worth considering. In many complex scenarios, a combination of both is ideal — a Will to handle personal items and residual matters, and a Trust to manage significant or sensitive assets.

THANK YOU! 

Thank you for exploring **Trusts Made Easy: Smart Tools to Save Tax, Secure Wealth & Protect Family**. I hope this book has provided you with valuable insights into the world of private trusts.

If you wish to further explore concepts related to estate planning, financial management, and tax-efficient structures, I encourage you to continue learning and staying informed.

Your feedback is invaluable. If you found this guide helpful, I would appreciate your thoughts and insights. Constructive feedback helps improve future editions and enhances the knowledge-sharing process.

For any academic discussions or clarifications, you may connect with me at:

Email: mlchhajerca@gmail.com

Thank you once again for your time and interest in this subject. I hope this knowledge empowers you to make informed financial decisions with clarity and confidence.

If you liked this book, do recommend it to your clients, friends, or colleagues who may benefit from understanding trust structures.